Insects, Spiders and Worms

Children's Science & Nature

BABY PROFESSOR

EDUCATION KIDS

Speedy Publishing LLC
40 E. Main St. #1156
Newark, DE 19711
www.speedypublishing.com

Insects are tiny animals with at least six legs and a hard shell. Most insects have wings and antennae.

Color Me!

grasshopper

grasshopper

grasshopper

Color Me!

wasp

wasp   wasp

wasp   wasp

Color Me!

mosquito

mosquito mosquito

mosquito mosquito

Color Me!

honeybee

honeybee

honeybee

Color Me!

caterpillar

caterpillar

caterpillar

Color Me!

ant

Color Me!

ladybug

ladybug ladybug

ladybug ladybug

Color Me!

spider

spider spider

spider spider

Color Me!

bug

bug bug bug

bug bug bug

Color Me!

earthworm

earthworm

earthworm

Color Me!

snail

snail snail snail

snail snail snail

Color Me!

butterfly

butterfly butterfly

butterfly butterfly

Color Me!

dragonfly

dragonfly

dragonfly

Color Me!

fly

fly fly fly

fly fly fly

Color all the
insects on the
next pages.

Visit
BABY PROFESSOR
EDUCATION KIDS
www.BabyProfessorBooks.com
to download Free Baby Professor eBooks
and view our catalog of new and exciting
Children's Books